Set design by Anna Louizos

Photo by Carol Rosegg

A scene from Manhattan Ensemble Theater's production of *The Castle*.
(*Left to right: Sean McCourt, William Atherton and Sarab Gurfield.*)

FRANZ KAFKA'S
THE CASTLE

ADAPTED BY
DAVID FISHELSON
AND AARON LEICHTER

FROM A DRAMATIZATION BY
MAX BROD

★

DRAMATISTS
PLAY SERVICE
INC.

2

"Surely I haven't made this journey for no reason."

—*K, The Castle*

ABOUT THE SCRIPT

Since its inception in 2000, Manhattan Ensemble Theater ("MET") had always hoped to have a dramatization of Franz Kafka's magnificent novel *The Castle* kick off a season. While Kafka's earlier novel *The Trial* had been dramatized frequently (most notably by Andre Gide, Jean-Louis Barrault, Orson Welles, Harold Pinter, Peter Weiss and Garland Wright), the equally well-regarded *The Castle* had received scant attention from the world's dramatists. Yes, there'd been a film with Maximilian Schell in the late 1960s, but our best research efforts turned up no versions for the stage.

By early 2001, we thought we'd need about two more years to develop a new dramatization: from commissioning a writer, to workshopping various drafts, to polishing the final product. Instead, to our astonishment, we discovered in the spring of 2001 that Max Brod himself had written a stage version of Kafka's final masterpiece. Brod was, of course, Kafka's best friend and editor, and the man who refused Kafka's deathbed request that all his writings be burned. Brod's refusal to do his friend's bidding proved to be one of the great gains for world literature.

As editor, Brod had to go through literally roomfuls of unfinished material: ordering and renumbering chapters, creating titles, and in a few cases, pulling excerpts from Kafka's diaries. The editing was particularly arduous with *The Castle,* given the degree to which the novel was unfinished at the time of Kafka's death.

It was a footnote in Mark Harman's wonderful translation of *The Castle* (Schocken Books, 1998) that alerted us to the existence of the Brod stage play. No version in English could be found, though we learned that Ingmar Bergman had directed it in Stockholm in 1953 (in Swedish) and that the Habimah had produced it in Tel Aviv in the 1970s. Weeks of searching led to, of all places, the NYU library (just three blocks from the MET facility!), which had a version in German. Petra Lammers and MET literary manager Aaron Leichter did a literal translation into English, which Aaron and I then adapted.

4

What Aaron and I found was that Brod solved many of the more difficult structural obstacles which *The Castle* presents to the dramatist. He not only distilled the novel into ten dramatic scenes (we wound up with twelve), but most importantly, he provided the story with an ending. Brod found this ending in, of all places, *The Trial,* for he used Kafka's most famous parable — the "Before the Law" scene in *The Trial's* penultimate chapter — as a kind of dream-confrontation between K and the Castle authorities. Brod used a very truncated version of the parable, and then ended the play with K's funeral. We thought it more organic to the novel (and more dramatically interesting) to include the *majority* of the parable, transpose its setting to the Castle itself, and then wind up with the somewhat open-ended climax you'll read herein.

Any time one adds an ending to a text that had none to begin with, you risk playing with fire — or, at least, the ire of a novel's legion of admirers. As two of those admirers, Aaron and I have taken our lead from Max Brod: by using his basic idea, but also by giving his version of *The Castle* the ending *we* wished it to have ... here in 2002, in New York City, a very particular place in time, and history.

—*David Fishelson, co-adapter*

THE KAFKAESQUE

Few artists ever develop as singular a style as Franz Kafka. Even though Kafka wrote only three novels and a few dozen short stories (almost none of which were published in his lifetime), his work is so uniquely haunting and familiar that his name inspired an adjective: Kafkaesque. A dictionary might define "Kafkaesque" as "any work marked by surreal logic of menacing proportions." But any definition misses the details that make Kafka's work so rewarding.

Kafka's stories take place in a universe that follows the logic of dreams. Time slips away, distances stretch and bend, people change personalities in an instant, and humans mutate overnight. Yet, as we do in dreams, his characters take these distortions in stride. This casual acceptance of the surreal hints at a shadowy world behind our own. In this world, everyone else knows what's going on, though they won't explain themselves. These people are petty, officious and self-important, but they're also somehow average, even boring, which ironically makes them more ominous. In Kafka's nightmare landscape, the most pedestrian objects and events become the most frightening.

Yet the tone is one not of danger but of guilt. Almost all of the characters assume they must be guilty of something. The happy ones don't care, and the foolish ones are proud. It falls to the protagonist to try to do something about it. These heroes are the most important characteristic of the Kafkaesque, though they are often left out of the definition. Even though they are aware that they don't fit in, fitting in is what they desire most. These heroes are almost anonymous: some have no name at all, while others, like the hero of *The Castle,* are known only by an initial. And they all strive with incredible, even stubborn, intensity to penetrate the mysteries of this world and relieve themselves of the burden of guilt.

Ultimately, however, this is impossible. Kafka's work might be summed up as the unstoppable force of the spirit meeting the immovable object of reality, except that Kafka believes that this force must eventually fail because it is human. But of all his writings, *The Castle* is the only one to provide a kind of solution, a suggestion that his art is not wholly pessimistic. In Kafka's earlier works, the hero's failure was complete. In *The Castle,* written two years before Kafka's death, K remains defiant until the end. His strength earns the reader's admiration and makes him tragic rather than pathetic. *The Castle* is one of the great tragedies of the twentieth century, not because it accepts that the unseen forces of the Kafkaesque will defeat us (though they certainly will), but because it suggests that we will continue to struggle. And that, Kafka implies, is itself a victory.

—*Aaron Leichter, co-adapter*

This adaptation of THE CASTLE received its world premiere by Manhattan Ensemble Theater (David Fishelson, Artistic Director) in New York City on January 8, 2002. It was directed by Scott Schwartz; the set design was by Anna Louizos; the lighting design was by Howell Binkley; the sound design was by Jon Weston; the costume design was by Miguel Angel Huidor; and dramaturgy was by Aaron Leichter. The cast was as follows:

K .... William Atherton
BARNABAS .... E.J. Carroll
FRIEDA .... Catherine Curtin
OLGA .... Mireille Enos
INNKEEPER'S WIFE .... Gina Ferrall
MOMUS / INNKEEPER .... Sean McCourt
JEREMIAH .... Jim Parsons
TEACHER .... Steven Rosen
MAYOR / GATEKEEPER .... Raynor Scheine
ARTHUR .... Grant James Varjas
ERLANGER / MANOR INNKEEPER .... Dan Ziskie
PEASANTS .... Ensemble
KLAMM'S SERVANTS .... Ensemble
Understudies .... Ian Pfister, Sarah Gurfield

CHARACTERS

K — a stranger between 35 and 50; intelligent, with sensitive features, not in great health

INNKEEPER — innkeeper of the Bridge Inn; by turns arrogant and fearful, clean-shaven

INNKEEPER'S WIFE — his wife, hard and tough

ARTHUR, JEREMIAH — twins, or near-twins, the two assistants; young men, both slender, in ill-fitting clothes, perhaps both with goatees

BARNABAS — the messenger from the Castle; a large man, open, friendly, innocent but worn-out by work

OLGA — Barnabas' sister; pretty, her features show more bitterness than those of her brother

MANOR INNKEEPER — middle-aged, bored, with a thick moustache

FRIEDA — the barmaid at the Manor House; sexy, confident, hard-featured, sensual

THE MAYOR — ill, 60s, wheelchair-bound, very soothing-but-droning voice

THE TEACHER — narrow-shouldered, bespectacled, very condescending

COACHMAN — a peasant sleigh driver

MOMUS — goateed, well-dressed, arrogant village secretary to Klamm

ERLANGER — an important middle-aged Castle official, bearded/goateed, gray-haired

SECOND COACHMAN — like the other coachman, perhaps bearded

THE GATEKEEPER — a large man with a long Tartaric beard.

SCENE BREAKDOWN

Scene 1: Bar of the Inn by the Bridge, night

Scene 2: Same location, next morning; then night

Scene 3: Outside and Inside the Manor House

Scene 4: Attic of the Bridge Inn, morning

Scene 5: The Mayor's Home, afternoon

Scene 6: Attic of the Bridge Inn, evening

Scene 7: Outside the Manor House, night; then dawn

Scene 8: Inside and Outside the Manor House, dawn

Scene 9: In Barnabas' Home, day

Scene 10: In the Manor House, night

Scene 11: Outside the Manor House, just before dawn

Scene 12: In a Sleigh, same time

In New York City, in 2002, the play was performed without an intermission.

THE CASTLE

Scene 1

A curtain conceals most of the stage, leaving at least a four-foot deep apron in front of the curtain. Sounds of snowstorm, wind. House lights fade out. The curtain opens enough to show K stopped for a moment, facing away from the audience, staring into the misty darkness. Snow falls on K. The curtain opens fully to reveal a desolate, wintry landscape, and in the middle of it all, a strange object: an open cubical frame large enough to hold several people, set on a turntable for easy rotation. K approaches this box, raises his hand and knocks. Though he knocks on open air, we hear the sound as if it were a big wooden door. At this, the snow stops, and people flood the stage, transforming the box into ...

The Bar of the Inn by the Bridge. There is a bar along one "wall," a table and several chairs, and a painting of the Castle. The storm is still heard, but outside now. At a table sit three Peasants, with beers, silent. The Innkeeper serves them. The Innkeeper's Wife is drying glasses. All wear coats indoors. K comes in from the cold, stamping his feet at the entrance. He stands there in a thin coat, shivering, a bit of snow on his head. Everyone stares at him. He stares back.

K. Can I stay here for the night? *(Silence.)* I've been walking for some time, and it got dark all of a sudden. *(More silence.)* I was hoping to make it up the hill — to the Castle — before nightfall but ... *(Still no one speaks.)* Is this place an inn or not?

INNKEEPER. Yes, it's an inn.

K. And people stay here? *(No answer.)* From time to time?

INNKEEPER. I don't have any rooms free.

K. But there's a storm outside.

INNKEEPER. I don't have any beds. Unless you want to sleep on the floor.

K. *(Not understanding.)* On the floor — ?

INNKEEPER. ... Or there's a straw mattress out in the corridor.

K. All right. *(Looks around, not sure where to go.)* You said it's — ?

INNKEEPER. *(Nodding toward a door.)* In the corridor.

K. In the corridor. *(K nods his thanks, heads for the door, watches the others watch him — exits. A moment passes. He reenters, laboriously dragging a straw mattress and a horse blanket. All watch him quietly. K makes his "bed" in the middle of the room. He stops briefly to look up at all of them. As if defending his action.)* It was too cold ... in the corridor ... *(Silence.)* ... Well, good night. *(He throws himself exhausted onto the straw mattress, face towards the corner, curls up, begins to fall asleep. After watching the sleeping K for a moment, the three Peasants confer in whispers, and then one of them gets up from his place and anxiously whispers in the Innkeeper's ear. The Innkeeper shakes his head, but the Peasant urgently reiterates his whispered point, then gives the Innkeeper a nudge in K's direction. Reluctantly, the Innkeeper goes over and stands next to K's mattress.)*

INNKEEPER. I'm sorry but you have to get up.

K. *(Jerks out of sleep.)* What — ?

INNKEEPER. You have to get up.

K. What's the matter — ?

INNKEEPER. This inn belongs to the Castle — the whole village does.

K. What does that have to do with —

INNKEEPER. Nobody can stay here without a permit. And you apparently don't have a permit, or at least you haven't shown it to anyone.

K. *(Still groggy.)* What do you mean I need a permit to stay here?

INNKEEPER. You need a permit to stay here. *(Some of the Peasants nod.)*

K. So I'll have to get this permit.

INNKEEPER. From whom sir?

K. From the Castle of course.

INNKEEPER. You want to get a permit from the Castle — at this hour?

K. Is that impossible?

INNKEEPER. You're joking.

K. If it's impossible then why'd you wake me up?

INNKEEPER. *(Angrily.)* How dare you!

K. *(Taken aback.)* What did I — ?

INNKEEPER. I insist that you respect the Castle's authority! I only woke you up to tell you that you have to leave this inn immediately!

K. *(Quietly but firmly.)* But I was hired by the Castle to come here. I've been hired as a land-surveyor.

FIRST PEASANT. *(Under his breath, to the others.)* Land-surveyor?

K. I have two assistants coming tomorrow in a carriage — or maybe they'll need a sleigh, with this snow ... I purposely chose to walk here rather than take transportation, but in doing so I got lost, and that's why I arrived so late. I know without being harassed by you that I can't show up at the Castle at night, so I chose to accept these simple accommodations. Now if you don't mind, I suggest that you leave me in peace here and allow me to get some sleep. *(K stares at the Innkeeper, who simply stares back. Finally, K turns towards the stove, tries to go back to sleep.)*

SECOND PEASANT. *(To the others.)* Land-surveyor?

THIRD PEASANT. What do we need a land-surveyor for?

FIRST PEASANT. Stay out of it —

INNKEEPER. I'll find out. *(Approaches a 1920s-era telephone, which hangs just offstage, pulls out a receiver attached to a long pull-cord, and cranks the offstage lever.)* Hello. The Caretaker, please ... He's asleep? Well there's a stranger staying at the Inn by the Bridge. Yes a complete stranger ... yes ... Well, he says that — *(Keeps talking quietly.)*

K. What are you saying to them?

INNKEEPER. — then *(Loud again.)* why don't you inquire at the Central Bureau if a land-surveyor really is expected... ! Thank you! *(Hangs up with annoyance.)*

K. *(To Innkeeper.)* I'm not pretending to be a land-surveyor.

INNKEEPER. I didn't say that. *(Long silence. The telephone rings.*

The Innkeeper picks it up, listens, hangs up, turns toward K.)

INNKEEPER. As I suspected: There's been no request for a land-surveyor. You're a liar, sir. Maybe worse. *(Two of the Peasants rise from the table and make a move towards K, who stares at them in astonishment. The phone rings again, stopping them.)* Yes? *(Listening on the phone — everyone else standing still.)* The department head himself said … *(Hangs up, looks at K.)* Perhaps … they made a mistake.

K. *(Stunned.)* That's all you have to say?

INNKEEPER. *(Stiffly.)* Well I imagine that perhaps an apology or expression of regret may be appropriate. Unless you don't require one at this time.

K. *(Waving him off.)* No. Thank you, just … go away for now. *(The Innkeeper remains standing there, staring. A pause.)* But thank you. *(The Innkeeper's Wife sets a basin and soap down before K, hands him a towel. He nods his thanks. The Innkeeper still hasn't moved — something's on his mind. K washes his face, then finally looks up. Drying his face.)* Yes — ?

INNKEEPER. I'd like to offer you a better room — my own if you want.

K. Why would you do that?

INNKEEPER. You're a guest of the Castle, acknowledged as such. *(The Peasants mutter amongst themselves.)*

FIRST PEASANT. He's actually employed —

SECOND PEASANT. As a land-surveyor —

THIRD PEASANT. Can he do us harm, then — ?

FIRST PEASANT. That's ridiculous —

INNKEEPER. *(Overlapping.)* I await your orders sir, if you have any. *(K dries off, hands Innkeeper the towel.)*

K. Just turn off the light, please. *(The Innkeeper seems frozen with indecision. K raises an eyebrow.)* The light — ? *(The Innkeeper — after a moment — snaps out of it, takes the towel, then reaches for the lamp. Blackout.)*

Scene 2

Same location, next morning, a sunny day. Innkeeper and K only. The Castle is seen through the back wall window in the distance, high on the hill. The storm is long over. As K gets up, stretches and puts on his overcoat, the Innkeeper approaches, holding out a guestbook and pen.

INNKEEPER. Good morning, sir. A moment please —
K. Yes?
INNKEEPER. Could I get your signature in the guestbook?
K. *(Takes the pen. While signing:)* How long a walk is it up the hill? *(Hands the pen back.)*
INNKEEPER. *(Looking at the signature.)* "K"?
K. How long a walk is it up the hill?
INNKEEPER. That's it? Just the letter "K"? *(K frowns at the Innkeeper's non-response, then impatiently turns to leave. The Innkeeper circles K, stops him.)* I would like to request ... that you excuse our impoliteness from last night.
K. *(Ignoring the request.)* My assistants will arrive soon. Will you be able to accommodate them here?
INNKEEPER. Of course, sir. *(Suddenly confused.)* But won't they be staying with you up at the Castle?
K. That hasn't been decided yet. First I have to find out what kind of work they have for me. Maybe I'll have things to do down here in the Village. In that case we'll stay here. Maybe I won't even like the accommodations up there. In the Castle. I'd like to keep my options open.
INNKEEPER. *(Quietly.)* You don't know the Castle.
K. *(With rising confidence.)* Perhaps, but they seem to know how to hire the right land-surveyor, wouldn't you say? *(Turns and looks out the window.)* Can I get a sleigh to take me up there?
INNKEEPER. I don't think any sleighs are available, sir.
K. But there must be four feet of snow on the ground.

INNKEEPER. It's not that.

K. Not what?

INNKEEPER. It's not the amount ...

K. Of sleighs?

INNKEEPER. Of snow.

K. But why can't I get a sleigh? *(No answer.)* Well if I have to, I'll walk.

INNKEEPER. It certainly is a long walk, sir.

K. Yes, and if I remain here talking to you, it'll feel longer still. Good day! *(K steps downstage, out of the inn. The Innkeeper stares after him. Lights down. A time transition, briefly, as two cast members spin the cube counterclockwise and K walks clockwise around it. As the cube spins, the Innkeeper stands still, staring straight ahead, so that when the spinning stops, both men have returned to their original positions. Lights change to night. The lamp is lit. The winds seem to be howling outside again. The Peasants sit at the table. The Innkeeper's Wife brings in beer. K enters, exhausted. The Innkeeper approaches him, holding a plate of food. To the Innkeeper.)* It's odd that the main street doesn't lead to the Castle, isn't it? I mean, it approaches the hill but suddenly turns away. You can always see the Castle just in front of you but you can't reach it. I kept walking ... but this village doesn't seem to have an end. I must have walked for hours. An old driver finally offered me a ride in his sleigh, but when I asked him to take me to the Castle, he just laughed and drove away ... Now a whole day's wasted: my first day. It's extremely discouraging ... *(The Innkeeper offers the plate of food to K.)* No thank you, I'm not hungry. *(K sits. The two Assistants, Arthur and Jeremiah, enter playfully, throwing snowballs at each other. They walk over to K, arms locked together, and salute him. K just stares at them. They stop saluting, stare back.)*

K. Who are you?

THE PAIR. Your assistants.

K. My assistants?

THE PAIR. Yes. Those assistants.

INNKEEPER. *(Popping up in between them.)* They are your assistants.

K. *(After a pause.)* They're not my assistants. I saw them in the Village. Somebody called one of you "Arthur" or something ...

16

You've been sent by the Castle, haven't you? To supervise me ... Where are *my* assistants? *(The Assistants look at each other and with gestures show they don't understand what he wants.)* Well ... where have you put the equipment?

THE PAIR. We don't have any equipment.

K. And what do you know about land surveying?

THE PAIR. Not a thing, sir!

K. Of course. Well, sit down — Innkeeper! Beer for those two. Sit. *(The Assistants sit on either side of K.)* Now this won't do: you two looking the same. How am I going to be able to tell you two apart?

THE PAIR. People usually manage to distinguish us quite well.

K. Yes, I'm sure they do, but *I* can't. I may have to call you both Arthur.

JEREMIAH. But I'm Jeremiah.

K. It doesn't matter. You'll both be equally responsible for every job I give you.

ARTHUR. But that'll be very unpleasant for us.

K. Of course it will. Now answer me — without any nonsense — can you get me a sleigh to take me up to the Castle? *(The Assistants don't answer. They look at each other. They look back at K. Finally Arthur speaks.)*

ARTHUR. Certainly.

JEREMIAH. Don't say "certainly." You know it's impossible —

K. *(Erupting suddenly.)* What do you mean it's impossible?!

ARTHUR. *(To K.)* He's right, no stranger can get into the Castle without permission.

K. And where do I get this permission?

ARTHUR. Maybe from ... the Castle Administration? I don't know —

K. Then let's phone them right now — *(They don't budge.)* Both of you! *(They rush speedily towards the phone, tripping over each other, fighting for the receiver. Jeremiah finally wins — he holds it in his hand, cranks the lever, listens.)*

JEREMIAH. Hello? Castle Administration? — *(Pause.)* Arthur and Jeremiah here, the Assistants —

ARTHUR. *(Overlapping.)* — the assistants to the new Land-surveyor. He'd like to know if he can come to the Castle. *(Pause.)*

THE PAIR. *(To K.)* He says "no".

K. Let me talk to them — *(K grabs the phone, as the three Peasants, the Innkeeper and his Wife, and the two Assistants all crowd around him.)*

K. Hello — hello —

FIRST PEASANT. They won't answer —

K. Can I have some quiet, please? — *(Stays at the phone, listening; his expression suddenly becomes calmer, as we hear the sound K describes.)* What an unusual sound ... I never ... Like children's voices. Humming. No ... Singing ... From far away ... Now it's one sound. As if it wants to penetrate ... beyond ... I'm not sure ...

INNKEEPER. *(Tugs on his shirt.)* Herr K —

K. Not now! *(The heavenly sound stops.)*

VOICE ON THE PHONE. *(Gruff.)* This is Oswald. Who's speaking?

K. Hello. This is, uh ...

VOICE OF OSWALD. Yes? Who is it? I'd like less telephoning from down there!

THE PAIR. *(Whispering to K.)* It's the assistant to the Land-surveyor.

K. It's the assistant to the Land-surveyor.

VOICE OF OSWALD. What? Who? Land-surveyor? What?

K. Why don't you ask the Department Head?

VOICE OF OSWALD. *(Muffled speaking; pause.)* Ah yes, the Land-surveyor. Which assistant are you?

THE PAIR. *(Whispering to K.)* Joseph.

K. Joseph.

VOICE OF OSWALD. Joseph? But the assistants are called — *(Muffled speaking again.)* — Arthur and Jeremiah —

K. Those are the new assistants.

VOICE OF OSWALD. No, they're the old ones.

K. They're the new ones. I'm the old one — the one who came today, to join the Land-surveyor.

VOICE OF OSWALD. No!

K. *(Taken aback.)* Then who am I?

VOICE OF OSWALD. You're ... *(Long pause; then in a lower voice.)* You are the old assistant. *(Another pause.)* What do you want?

K. When can my master come to the Castle?

VOICE OF OSWALD. What?

K. When can my master come to the Castle?

VOICE OF OSWALD. You know the answer to that.

K. Well what is the answer? *(The click of a hang-up. K cranks the phone two times …)* Hello? Hello?? *(He slowly walks away, still holding the receiver. The Innkeeper tugs on K's shirt again.)*

INNKEEPER. Herr K —

K. *(Still in a daze.)* What…?

INNKEEPER. A messenger's here for you. *(Barnabas — who entered behind the crowd during the phone call — towers above them atop a chair, holding aloft a letter from the Castle.)*

BARNABAS. My name is Barnabas. *(He descends, losing his gravity as he stumbles a little, and hands K the letter. K opens it.)*

K. *(Reading the letter.)* It's from Castle Bureau Number 10. *(The group crowds around K again.)* "Dear Sir: As you know, you've been accepted into the employment of the Castle. Your immediate supervisor is the Mayor of the Village, who will introduce you to everything relating to your work and to whom you are accountable. Nevertheless, I will keep my eye on you as well. Barnabas, the carrier of this letter, will check with you from time to time to determine your wishes and communicate them to me. You will always find me prepared to help you insofar as that is possible. It is my desire to have contented workers. SIGNED: The Board of the Tenth Bureau." — The signature … is illegible. — *(Looking up at them all.)* This is a very important letter. — The first step has been taken. I announced myself, and I was accepted. A success.

INNKEEPER. My highest congratulations.

K. But wait: The letter is inconsistent. It says here "your immediate supervisor is the Mayor of the Village … " Not someone in•the Castle, but someone in the *Village*. And here: "You will always find me prepared to help you insofar as that is possible … " What does that mean: that he *is* empowered, or not? Why is there any layer of authority between me and the Castle — ? *(K looks at them all — no one answers.)* Well, whom do I actually work for then? The Village or the Castle?

INNKEEPER. There's no difference between the Village and the Castle.

K. That's ridiculous — *(To himself.)* … unless they're going to insist that I become a Villager first — put down roots ... But that could take forever — *(Holding up the letter, to Barnabas.)* Have you read this?

BARNABAS. No sir, I just got the order to bring it here, wait until it was read, then return with a verbal or written answer.

K. A written answer is unnecessary. Please convey to — *(Looks at the letter.)* what's his name, I can't read the damn signature —

BARNABAS. Klamm.

K. Please convey to Herr Klamm my thanks for his recognition. I shall follow his wishes most faithfully but ... I ask him if he'd be good enough to receive me personally. In the Castle.

BARNABAS. May I repeat the message? I'm new, and it's important that I make no mistakes.

K. Yes —

BARNABAS. Written answer unnecessary. Please convey to ... — what's his name? I can't read the damn signature —

K. No, no, don't say that —

BARNABAS. *(Mechanically.)* I can't read the damn signature. No, no, don't say that — please convey to Herr Klamm my thanks for his recognition. I shall follow his wishes most faithfully but ... I ask him if he'd be good enough to receive me personally. In the ... In the ...

K. In the Castle.

BARNABAS. Do I have to say it that way, sir?

K. What's wrong with saying it that way?

BARNABAS. It's a new job, sir, and I ... that is ... *(K stares at Barnabas for a few moments, waiting for him to finish. Barnabas falls awkwardly silent. Tiredly.)* All right. You can leave ... "Barnabas"? That's your name?

BARNABAS. Yes sir. Barnabas. *(Barnabas nods, bows, exits. K stands in the middle of the room — folds and pockets the note. He looks from one face to the other — the Innkeeper, the Innkeeper's Wife, Assistants, Peasants — all simply stare back at him.)*

K. *(Quietly.)* Barnabas...? *(K swivels to the right, to the left. He appears to be — or feel — trapped. Now shouting after the departed messenger.)* Barnabas — ! *(Finally shoves his way through the crowd toward the exit.)* Wait for me — !

Scene 3

Outside — then inside — the Manor House Inn. The lights dim as K runs after Barnabas. They go around the cube as it rotates a quarter turn, so that the bar faces upstage, its back to the audience. Thus the audience will be able to see what happens behind and under the bar itself. Barnabas comes downstage, meeting his sister Olga. Lights back to full as K finally catches up.

K. Barnabas!

BARNABAS. *(Stops, turns.)* Sir — ?

K. The way it's written here doesn't make any sense — *(Pointing at the letter.)* It says that you'll check in with me "from time to time" ... But that's not enough. What if I have something urgent to tell the Castle?

BARNABAS. You could see if Herr Klamm will give me permission to come looking for you — at designated times, sir.

K. *(Very agitated.)* But that's not good enough either, Barnabas. *(Barnabas stares, not sure what to say.)* Are you going to see this Klamm person now?

BARNABAS. No sir, it's too late.

K. But don't you go back to the Castle at night?

BARNABAS. No, I sleep at my home here — in the Village.

K. But I thought —

BARNABAS. I only go there in the morning to receive my orders, sir.

K. But I was hoping ... that you could take me up there now. *(K raises his eyebrows hopefully, shivers. Barnabas wears a fearful expression.)*

BARNABAS. I'm not allowed to bring anyone with me, sir. Ever. *(K shivers some more, starts staring off into space. Olga whispers a suggestion in Barnabas's ear.)* If you like ... we live nearby — our house is simple, but you could stay the night.

K. Don't you have close connections to the Castle?

BARNABAS. No, I'm just a messenger, sir.

K. *(Looks at Olga.)* And is this your wife?

BARNABAS. No, it's my sister Olga. She has some work to do at the Manor House.

K. The "Manor House." What's that?

BARNABAS. *(Indicates behind him.)* This is the Manor House. *(Lights fade up on the interior of the Bar.)* It's the *other* inn in the Village, the second one, or the first, considering the quality. Officials from the Castle eat here when they have business in the Village. Sometimes they stay the night.

K. *(Rubbing his cold hands.)* There's probably a room here for me, then.

BARNABAS. I don't think so. The inn is reserved for Castle officials only.

K. *(With frustration.)* Look here, I've been hired by the Castle, it's not like I'm some … Besides, it's too cold to walk back.

BARNABAS. As I said, you could stay with us, sir. *(K hesitates, rubs his hands — he doesn't want to retreat from his goal tonight.)*

K. "Olga," right? Maybe you could help me get in here?

OLGA. I'll help you, Land-surveyor. *(K and Olga exchange a meaningful look.)*

BARNABAS. *(Bowing to K.)* If you'll allow me, sir, I'll go then. *(He gives Olga a worried look, then exits. The Manor Innkeeper emerges, blocking K's access to the inn.)*

MANOR INNKEEPER. *(To Olga.)* What does the Land-surveyor want here?

OLGA. He's escorting me.

MANOR INNKEEPER. I can only let him into the bar.

K. *(Taking the Manor Innkeeper aside.)* I'd like to spend the night here, if that's possible.

MANOR INNKEEPER. *(With a tired expression.)* Only officials from the Castle get to stay here.

K. I understand that's the rule. But you must have something …

MANOR INNKEEPER. I'd be delighted to accommodate you — but the rules are very strict. Only a stranger who doesn't know what's going on would talk about it the way you're doing. If somehow I let you stay the night, and by chance, you were discovered

— then I'd be lost. And you too would be lost. It may sound absurd, but that's the way it is.

K. *(Clutching the Manor Innkeeper's arm.)* I believe you completely. And I don't underestimate the importance of the rules — I just want to point out that I have valuable connections at the Castle, and I'm sure to establish even more valuable ones in the future. These connections would certainly protect you from any danger that could arise by your accommodating me here. You understand that, don't you?

MANOR INNKEEPER. I hear what you're saying … *(A pause.)*

K. Are there many officials from the Castle staying here tonight?

MANOR INNKEEPER. Just one: Herr Klamm.

K. *(Astonished.)* Herr Klamm!?

MANOR INNKEEPER. My respects to you. Good night. *(Exits into the inn.)*

K. *(To Olga.)* Klamm is here. What luck! *(Taking Olga's arm, they enter. Now the room is fully illuminated — Klamm's Servants, three of them, dressed in different colors than the Peasants earlier, sit against the walls, immediately focusing on Olga. Frieda is behind the bar. To Frieda.)* Is Herr Klamm here in the room? *(Olga laughs.)* Why are you laughing?

OLGA. I'm not laughing. *(But Olga does laugh, as she trades disdainful looks with Frieda. Then Olga enters the circle of Klamm's Servants — they put their hands on her waist and breasts.)*

FRIEDA. *(To K.)* You're not supposed to be in here, Land-surveyor.

K. How does everyone know that I'm — Who are you?

FRIEDA. Frieda, the barmaid here. — Do you know Olga well, Land-surveyor?

K. I've known Olga fifteen minutes. She's Barnabas' sister —

FRIEDA. You don't have to tell me anything about Barnabas and his repulsive family. See what I mean? *(She nods toward Olga. Klamm's Servants have started to surround her, undoing her hair, her blouse, and humming in a seductive/obscene way. Olga looks bored by it, but lets it happen.)*

K. That's funny. She seemed like such a nice girl before —

FRIEDA. That slut? — Look at those pigs —

K. Who are they?

FRIEDA. Klamm's people. It's the kind of scum I have to deal with here. How many times have I told him to leave them at the Castle ... But "Herr Klamm" doesn't give a damn what I have to put up with. He doesn't give a damn about me. *(She does a slow burn.)* I'll get them out myself then, right now — *(She grabs a horsewhip off the wall, moves toward the "orgy," who at first behave as if a new participant is approaching.)* In the name of Klamm, get into the stable! *(Cracks the whip.)* Everyone into the stable! *(She cracks the whip again. The Servants stop laughing, start moving quickly toward the exit along with Olga. Frieda follows, swinging and cracking the whip. K alone on the stage; steps can be heard. Moments later, Frieda returns. K looks at her, a little unsure of what to say. She laughs.)* You asked me if Klamm was here. The fact is, he only leaves his room when he's about to go back to the Castle.

K. You know him?

FRIEDA. Quite well — *(Looking K in the eye.)* — I'm his mistress.

K. *(Pause.)* Then that makes you a very important person — to me.

FRIEDA. Not just to you. I've got the position of barmaid here at the Manor House. I started out as a stablemaid, at the other inn, the one by the bridge. I'm glad to be the barmaid now.

K. Well you've come up in the world then, haven't you?

FRIEDA. I'd say so.

K. Listen to me — Someday you might find the help of a man like myself useful. Someone who's fighting to advance himself, like you are. Can we talk about it sometime? Privately?

FRIEDA. I don't know what you're after. *(Pause.)*

MANOR INNKEEPER. *(Voice offstage, approaching.)* Frieda — !

FRIEDA. Do you want to take me away from Klamm, for heaven's sake?

MANOR INNKEEPER. *(Closer now.)* Frieda!

FRIEDA. *(To K.)* All right. When can I talk to you?

K. *(Pleased he's gotten through to her.)* Can I spend the night here?

FRIEDA. Yes. Now hide! *(Just as the Manor Innkeeper enters, Frieda pushes K down to hide him behind the bar. He is still visible to the audience.)*

MANOR INNKEEPER. Where's the Land-surveyor?

FRIEDA. *(Looks around.)* He must have left.

MANOR INNKEEPER. I would've seen him outside, no one's come out.

FRIEDA. Well he isn't here.

MANOR INNKEEPER. He can't stay the night. You know that. Where could he have gone? Maybe he's hiding.

FRIEDA. I don't think he's that brave. Maybe he's — under the bar? *(Kneels down to K, kisses him quickly on the lips, jumps back up.)* Nope, not there. *(K is surprised by the kiss. After he recovers, he starts playing along, caressing her leg.)*

MANOR INNKEEPER. The rules apply to you too, Fräulein, as well as to me. You're responsible for the bar. I'll check the rest of the house — good night. *(Exits. Frieda waits a few seconds after he departs ... then suddenly she ducks under the bar, grabs K's face and kisses him deeply. He responds by grabbing and crushing her body to his. They rip at each others' clothes hungrily, devouring each other in passionate kissing on the face, the neck, the chest. They drag each other down upstage of the bar, out of the audience's sight. Sounds of lovemaking in the dark .... The lights come back up to the sound of birds — it's dawn.)*

OFFSTAGE VOICE. *(Commanding.)* Frieda!

K. *(Startled, his head emerging above the bar.)* Who's that?

FRIEDA. *(Pulling herself up and dressing herself, she whispers.)* It's Klamm.

K. Where is he?

FRIEDA. *(Pointing towards a door.)* The next room.

K. The next — *(Alarmed, he stands up — his pants around his ankles — puts them on, hopping.)*

FRIEDA. Why? I'm not going back to him now —

K. Frieda, don't be hasty —

FRIEDA. "Hasty": what does that mean?

K. Just that — let's not do something we might possibly —

FRIEDA. No. I've had enough. *(Frieda gets up, buttons her blouse, moves towards Klamm's door.)*

K. Stop! What're you —

FRIEDA. *(Banging on the door with her fist, to Klamm.)* I'm with the Land-surveyor, Klamm! How do you like *that*!

K. *(Grabbing his head in frustration.)* What're you doing! We'll be ruined!

FRIEDA. Not you — just me.

K. But Klamm's the one who —

FRIEDA. You worry too much. *(Laughs suddenly at something over K's shoulder.)*

K. What — ? *(Turns around. Sees the two Assistants, who've suddenly appeared, sitting on the bar, using their hands as binoculars to watch Frieda and K.)* What are you doing here?

ARTHUR. We came looking for you.

JEREMIAH. You didn't come back to the inn.

ARTHUR. We went to Barnabas's.

JEREMIAH. We finally found you here.

ARTHUR. We sat here the whole night.

JEREMIAH. Our duties aren't easy.

K. You've been watching us —

ARTHUR. *(Smiling.)* Most of the night, sir —

JEREMIAH. *(Smiling too.)* Doing our *job* —

ARTHUR. Thank you very much —

K. Get out!

THE PAIR. But —

K. *(Rising with a terrible fury.)* Get OUT!! NOW!! OUT OUT OUT — !! *(Suddenly, the Servants, Manor Innkeeper, and Olga come pouring in. Olga's clothes are ripped and dirty: She must hold them up, or else be naked.)*

OLGA. *(Tearfully to K, as she passes him.)* Why didn't you take me home — ! *(Indicating Frieda.)* — So you could be with *her?*

FRIEDA. Look who's talking — now get out —

OLGA. You're the one who has to get out.

MANOR INNKEEPER. *(To K.)* Land-surveyor! *(To Frieda.)* I knew it! I warned you, Fräulein.

FIRST SERVANT. Good timing, Land-surveyor!

SECOND SERVANT. Stayed here the night. He thinks he's better than us!

THIRD SERVANT. Frieda too!

FRIEDA. Come on, Land-surveyor, you're with me now —

K. Where are we going — ?

FRIEDA. To the Bridge Inn, of course. The Innkeeper's Wife is like a mother to me — *(The Servants start to block her way. One of them takes hold of her shoulder —)*

SECOND SERVANT. She always pushed us around!

THIRD SERVANT. Now it's *her* turn, all right — !

26

FRIEDA. Arthur! Jeremiah! The whip! *(The whip is suddenly slapped into her hand; she raises it … Frieda chases the Servants, pulling K along with her. The Assistants follow, laughing. During the chase, the set is rotated so that one corner points at the audience.)*

Scene 4

An Attic room in the Bridge Inn. Morning. A bed is off to one side, while a dressing screen hides the back corner. On the wall a picture of another, obviously different castle. K still in bed, just waking up. Frieda sits by his side, wearing an apron, gently brushing the hair from K's brow.

FRIEDA. Good morning … darling.
K. *(Lifting himself up on one arm, groggily.)* How long did I sleep?
FRIEDA. The whole day and night. It's morning now. I haven't slept this well in years. *(K looks around, trying to remember.)*
K. And Klamm's letter? *(Looks around anxiously.)* Where is the letter from Klamm —
FRIEDA. Calm yourself. *(The letter hangs from the wall. K immediately goes to it, lifts it tenderly … slowly returns to Frieda's side, sits on bed. Frieda suddenly smothers K with a passionate kiss, wrapping her arms around him. The Assistants, sensing a show, peer around the screen. K notices and stands in shock at this new reappearance of the Assistants. As he does, Klamm's letter slips out of his hands. Frieda picks it up to protect it for him and keeps it in her hands for the whole scene.)*
K. What are you doing here?
FRIEDA. Like us, they have nowhere else to sleep. *(K eyes them for a moment.)*
K. Gentlemen, you may have to sleep here, but you needn't watch every move I make.
THE PAIR. But that's our job.
K. Well, *(Indicating himself and Frieda.)* this is not.

THE PAIR. It's not?

K. No. Of course not. *(Turning back to the twins.)* Wait for me downstairs.

THE PAIR. We could wait here.

K. *(Calmly.)* But I don't want you to wait here.

JEREMIAH. *(Nudging Arthur.)* He wants to be alone.

ARTHUR. *(Nudging Jeremiah.)* Yes, that goes for you too.

JEREMIAH. *(Pushing Arthur.)* But I said it *first* —

K. *(Raising his voice.)* NOW! *(Both quickly turn to exit and bump into the Innkeeper's Wife, who shoves them aside as she enters. The tough woman looks grumpy and gives K a withering glance.)*

INNKEEPER'S WIFE. I've been waiting outside for a long time, Land-surveyor. I need to speak with you.

K. Yes, madam.

INNKEEPER'S WIFE. It's about our little Frieda. I love her and care for her, Land-surveyor — *(Holding out her arms to Frieda.)* — my angel. *(Frieda leaves K and lets herself be wrapped up in the Innkeeper's Wife's embrace, sitting on her lap, her head on her chest.)*

K. I love her too, madam. Perhaps you'll be reassured then when I tell you that I think Frieda and I should be married — and the sooner the better.

Frieda. *(In shock.)* Darling — !

K. Unfortunately, I won't be able to replace what she's lost because of me: her position at the Manor House, her friendship with Klamm —

INNKEEPER'S WIFE. *(Snorting.)* Hm, then it's what I suspected — in spite of this "marriage proposal" of yours, you're not in fact offering her any guarantees.

K. *(Confused by this remark.)* But that's what I hope to solve by speaking with Herr Klamm in person — indeed, I hope to meet with him before the wedding.

FRIEDA. *(Rising off the woman's lap.)* That's impossible —

K. *(To Frieda.)* And if I can't, you may have to, Frieda —

FRIEDA. But I can't do it either. How can you even *think* that Klamm will talk to me? *Or* you?

K. But he *might* talk to you —

FRIEDA. To *me?* Are you insane!? *(She turns toward the Innkeeper's Wife.)* Look what he's asking for!

INNKEEPER'S WIFE. *(To K.)* You're a strange person.

K. Why is that?

INNKEEPER'S WIFE. I don't belong to the Castle, so perhaps you don't take me seriously —

FRIEDA. *(To the Innkeeper's Wife.)* You're wrong, ma'am, the Land-surveyor respects you highly —

INNKEEPER'S WIFE. Then listen to me, Land-surveyor! You have to understand what we take for granted: that Herr Klamm will never speak to you and *can* never speak to you. Herr Klamm is a *gentleman from the Castle.* And you? You aren't from the Castle, you aren't from the Village, you're nothing. Even worse, you're a stranger: a man who's ruined our sweet little Frieda here, and who, unfortunately, we have to accept as her husband. A man like Klamm talking to you! He doesn't even speak to people from the Village. This was Frieda's great achievement — and mine too — *(Nodding proudly.)* — yes, I was Klamm's mistress as well, years ago! I can't understand how a girl who's actually had the honor of sharing his bed would've ... left the eagle, as it were ... to sleep with the worm —

K. You may be right, madam, that I'm a worm compared to a man like Klamm — *(Smiles, shakes his head.)* — but that's no reason for my *avoiding* Klamm. I just want to speak to him, face to face — about Freida, about my appointment as land-surveyor — to sort out whatever ambiguities might still remain —

INNKEEPER'S WIFE. I knew it. Marrying Frieda so you can get closer to Klamm —

K. Nonsense —

INNKEEPER'S WIFE. You've only been in the Village a couple of days, and already you want more than the natives!

K. No that's not true. I was hired by the Castle, and I have the right to speak to Klamm.

INNKEEPER'S WIFE. *Nothing* happens the way you're trying to do it, forcing your way in and so on. Why if it wasn't for Frieda I'd throw you out in the snow myself, right now! And *then* I'd like to see you find a bed anywhere in this Village — even in a doghouse!

K. Thank you for your kind words, madam, but I know a place where I can get a bed right now, if I wanted to —

FRIEDA and INNKEEPER'S WIFE. *(At the same time.)* Where?

K. With Barnabas.

INNKEEPER'S WIFE. *(Snorting.)* That scum! "With Barnabas" — see who the man hobnobs with! Of course he can get a bed there!

K. I don't know what sins the family of Barnabas has committed. But I do know that when you came in here, you were talking about love and care — yet all you've shown us is hatred and scorn. And if you think you can separate me from Frieda — well, you're going about it very cleverly, but I doubt you'll succeed … As far as this little room of yours goes, I can't tell if you've given it to me of your own free will, or whether the Castle insisted on it. Either way, I'm sure they'll find me new lodgings if you kick me out. No doubt then you'll be relieved, but no more so than I, madam, I assure you. *(Rises, heads for the exit.)* Now I really must go and see the Mayor. As you've no doubt heard, I came here on assignment —

INNKEEPER'S WIFE. *(Grabbing his sleeve.)* You're not only ignorant about the way things are done around here, but it's the kind of ignorance that can get a person into trouble —

K. *(Trying to go.)* Thank you, madam —

INNKEEPER'S WIFE. *(Gripping him tighter.)* What is it that you want from him, Land-surveyor?

K. I simply want to hear what my work will be. *(Raising his voice.)* Why should that seem so odd?

INNKEEPER'S WIFE. *(To Frieda.)* He's out of his mind, Frieda … *(To K.)* Do whatever you want, Land-surveyor — I tried. *(She exits.)*

K. What have I done? If I can't speak to Herr Klamm, then who? Who should I talk to? *(Frieda takes Klamm's letter off the wall. She reads:)*

FRIEDA. … "Dear sir, as you know, you've been accepted into the employment of the … Your immediate supervisor is the Mayor of the Village" …

K. What?

FRIEDA. Dear sir …

K. No! *(He snatches the letter from her hand and reads furiously.)* … who will introduce you to everything relating to your work and to whom you are accountable … The Mayor.

FRIEDA. Darling? *(K kisses Frieda hard and fast. He is overjoyed.)* K. Arthur, Jeremiah! *(They are there instantly.)* You're late! Come! The Mayor! *(The three exit briskly as Frieda stays behind, watching them leave.)*

Scene 5

The Mayor's home. The Mayor will eventually sit in a chair, his feet up on a footstool. K will eventually sit next to the Mayor in another chair. Betweeen the chairs, on a table, sits a model of the Castle. K is discovered helping the Mayor — 60-ish, ill — to his chair. As they converse, the Assistants carry boxes of files onstage and stack them.

MAYOR. Have a seat, have a seat, sir, and tell me your wishes. I'd like to hear them. I will do all that I can.
K. *(Remains standing.)* It's a simple case, sir: I've been hired to be a land-surveyor by the Castle, in connection with which I received this letter — *(Takes the letter from his pocket and shows it.)* — signed by Herr Klamm, Head of the Tenth Castle Bureau. The letter refers me to you, sir, the Mayor — and so I'm here to receive my instructions.
MAYOR. As you probably know, I've been informed about the case. Yet so far, I haven't arranged anything — firstly because I'm ill — and secondly: you didn't come for such a long time, I'd already assumed you'd given up on the issue. But now that you're here, I'm afraid I have some rather unpleasant news. As you say, you've been hired as the Land-surveyor. But unfortunately we don't need a land-surveyor. There wouldn't be the slightest bit of work for you to do here. The borders of our little territory are already marked down, and everything has been properly recorded. So why should we need a land-surveyor?
K. *(Long pause.)* I can only hope there's been some mistake.
MAYOR. No, unfortunately, it's as I've said.

K. That's not possible. Surely I haven't made this journey for no reason —

MAYOR. That's a different question, and one that isn't for me to decide. But I can explain how this miscommunication might've occurred. In an organization as large as the Castle's, sometimes one department decides one thing, while another decides something else. Neither knows about the other, and there's always the chance that confusion can arise. Obviously the Castle is highly efficient, so this kind of mishap only occurs with the pettiest of issues: such as your case for example —

K. For example —

MAYOR. Now regarding your commission, let me tell you what I think happened. A long time ago, when I'd been Mayor for only a few months, an order came down that a land-surveyor was to be called in. Of course, the order wasn't about you personally, because it was many years ago. I wouldn't have remembered it if I wasn't so ill and didn't have all this extra time to think about things like that. *(Turns toward the Assistants, who've finished stacking the boxes.)* Ah, the Assistants: would the two of you please look up in those boxes there, maybe you'll find the file. *(To K.)* I still kept things in order back then. I've stopped now — *(The Assistants begin making a mess of things: opening the boxes, sending papers fluttering around. After a while paper covers half of the room. All the while, the Mayor drones on.)*

MAYOR. As you can see, a great deal of work has been done here over the years. And this is only a small fraction of it. I stored most of it in the barn, but the majority of it has been lost, I'm afraid. *(To the Assistants.)* Look for something with the word "land-surveyor" underlined in blue pencil —

K. But how on earth did I get summoned here?

MAYOR. Your summons was carefully considered, that much I know. It was only certain auxiliary circumstances that intervened and confused things. I'll prove it to you: it's in the file —

THE PAIR. But the file can't be found.

MAYOR. Can't be found? *(Shouting, to Assistants.)* Please look more quickly! *(To K.)* Ah well … I can still tell you the story without the file. In replying to the order that I mentioned, we graciously answered that we didn't need a land-surveyor. But the answer didn't seem to have reached the original department, which I'll call A; instead they went to a different department, which I'll call B. At any rate, the head of department B wasn't satisfied with our answer. A lengthy correspondence developed. Finally the mistake was discovered by the Control Authority.

K. I'm glad you mention a Control Authority. It sounds from your description as though the organization has no central control whatsoever. *(The Assistants start having fun with the files. They build little paper airplanes, which they throw at each other. Laughter, stumbling, more scattering.)*

MAYOR. No central control? Only a stranger who doesn't know what's going on would talk about it that way. You see, there's a peculiar feature that's characteristic of the administrative apparatus. When an issue has been considered for a very long time, it can happen that suddenly, in a flash, from some unexpected place, a decision will arise that solves the problem immediately. It's as if the system was unable to bear the tension — the year-long or decade-long irritation caused by the affair — and because of this, a decision from within itself will have been made without the help of any of the employees. But the Control departments only realize this much later; we of course never hear anything about it. I don't know if a decision of this kind was made in your case. If so, then such an order would have been sent out to you. And then, yes, it's safe to say that you would have made the long journey for, as you say, "no reason." Does that make any sense?

K. *(Pulling out Klamm's letter.)* What about this letter that Herr Klamm sent to me?

MAYOR. *(Taking the letter.)* Klamm's letter is valuable. The signature seems to be real. But apart from that — *(Suddenly the Mayor notices — for the first time — the horrible mess the Assistants have made behind him.)* What are you doing?!

THE PAIR. We've been unable to find the file!

MAYOR. Ah — so it can't be found. Too bad. *(To K.)* But now you know the whole story. We don't really need the file anymore, and anyway it'll probably be found later on. *(Looks back down at Klamm's letter.)* This is a private letter, not an official one. That's clear from the salutation: "Dear Sir ... " *(Looks up.)* Obviously, a private letter from Klamm is more important than an official letter; but I don't think it means what you think it does.

K. Wait! So, according to you, I'm *not* employed as a land-surveyor?

MAYOR. Perhaps. But perhaps not.

K. Is everything here unclear and unsolvable?

MAYOR. Again, I can only say "perhaps." You may or may not be correct not to take communications from the Castle at face value. Of course, regarding all of this, considerations are needed, and I'll have to send a report to the Castle. Should there be a decision in your case, I'll send someone to inform you immediately. Will that be satisfactory? *(K — who's been standing the whole time — finally slumps into the chair next to the Mayor that had been offered him at the beginning of the scene. He rubs his brow anxiously.)*

K. I need to speak to someone in the Castle.

MAYOR. *(Not listening to him.)* One more thing: You can always turn to me in confidence —

K. I simply want a ride, some kind of transportation up the hill —

MAYOR. I won't say that you have a friend in me — because we're complete strangers — but I want to be of help to you in any way that I can —

K. If I could just be *taken* to the Castle —

MAYOR. There's only one thing I can't allow though: Since there's no land-surveying that needs to be done here, I'm afraid you won't be allowed to be employed as a land-surveyor. I'm sorry … *(K freezes, hand on brow; he slowly looks up at the Mayor.)*

K. Can Herr Klamm overrule that judgment?

MAYOR. Excuse me?

K. Can Klamm … *overrule* that judgment? The one you've just made.

MAYOR. Even if he were available for such a discussion, I hardly imagine that he would —

K. *(Walking the Mayor off the cube and grabbing the Mayor by the collar.)* I simply asked you if he *could*. Not if he would. *(The Mayor stares at K, blinking.)*

MAYOR. I suppose … I suppose that … Well, yes, I guess it's safe to presume that he has the power to do that. Again, I —

K. *(Letting the Mayor's collar go.)* Thank you sir. *(He pats down and smooths out the collar he's ruffled.)* I hope that your … health takes a turn for the better. *(K turns the the Mayor around and kick-push-es him offstage. K walks around and in front of the cube, while it's changed behind him.)*

Scene 6

Evening: K's Attic Room in the Inn at the Bridge. The Teacher stops K as he walks across the stage.

TEACHER. You must be the Land-surveyor.
K. I am. Who are you?
TEACHER. The Schoolteacher. The Mayor asked me to speak to you.
K. Did he? About what?
TEACHER. You were discourteous to his Honor. The Mayor is an extremely well-regarded personage in the Village, and he deserves to be treated with greater respect than you were able to muster.
K. I wasn't discourteous, I was disturbed!
TEACHER. I only learned about your rudeness, and his kind-ness, from a short protocol he dictated to me detailing the con-versation.
K. But I just came from there, how did you...? I didn't realize it was an official conversation.
TEACHER. It wasn't, it was only semi-official. And so is the pro-tocol. But now that it's written, it works against you and your case.
K. Fine, fine. Is that all?
TEACHER. No. The Mayor is afraid you might do something rash if your case takes too long to resolve. And while he can't speed up the Castle's decision on your behalf, he wants to make a gener-ous offer. He wants to offer you — provisionally, of course — the post of School Janitor. *(K stares down at the floor, unmoving.)* I objected, of course. I told him that until now a Janitor had been unnecessary. I had enough trouble with the children, I didn't want

to be bothered by a janitor as well. And I pointed out that you didn't know the work, and furthermore that since there were only two rooms in the school, you'd have to live, sleep, perhaps even cook in one of the classrooms. But the Mayor mentioned further that we'd gain the services of your wife and assistants in addition, so that perhaps the garden as well as the school might receive greater attention. I argued with him, and finally, unable to come up with anything else in your favor, he just laughed and said that since you're a land-surveyor after all, perhaps you'd be able to lay out the vegetable garden in a more orderly fashion. *(Slight humorless chuckle.)* Well, there's no arguing with a joke, so I came to you with the proposal.

K. Thank you sir, but you needn't have worried yourself to this extent. I have no intention of accepting the position.

TEACHER. Excellent. *(Rises, preparing to leave.)* I'll be on my way then.

FRIEDA. *(To the Teacher.)* Don't leave yet, sir — *(Pulls K into the room; the Teacher follows them.)* You have to accept his offer.

K. Don't be ridiculous —

FRIEDA. The Innkeeper's Wife wants you to leave here immediately.

K. Why, what's wrong?

FRIEDA. I don't know. She says that if you have such good connections with the Castle, then you should take advantage of them. Oh darling, if worse comes to worst, we can go away — what is there in the Village to keep us? Accept the offer, please — for now at least. I don't think we have a choice.

K. But ... It's beneath our contempt, Frieda —

TEACHER. *(Pulling out his watch.)* It's getting late.

FRIEDA. *(To the Teacher.)* That's why we've come to a decision sir. We'll take the position.

TEACHER. The post is only being offered to the Land-surveyor. He must speak for himself.

FRIEDA. He accepts — *(To K.)* — Don't you? *(K stares at her incredulously.)* I'll do the work. *(K now frowns at her ... After a few moments, he sighs, nods reluctantly.)*

K. All right —

TEACHER. Your salary, though, can only be considered after a month's trial.

FRIEDA. That's a bit harsh, isn't it, sir? Couldn't you advise the Village Council to grant us a small stipend: at the start, at least? We'll be newlyweds.

TEACHER. No. Representations to the Village Council can only be made if I give the word. And I can't. The position has been offered to the Land-surveyor only as a personal favor, and one can't push a favor like that too far.

K. I think you're wrong, sir. I think it's me who's doing the favor.

FRIEDA. *(To K.)* Don't start —

TEACHER. *(To K.)* Why do you say that? Our need for a janitor is about as urgent as our need for a land-surveyor.

K. That's what I mean. You're being forced to take me on against your will. Although it may cause you grave perturbation, you have to take me on. And when someone like you is compelled to take someone on, and the someone who is taken on allows himself to be taken on, then he is the one who is granting someone the favor.

TEACHER. *(Smiling.)* The only thing compelling someone here to take on someone there is the Mayor's generosity. I'd be careful not to tax that if I were you. *(Putting his hat on.)* You'll have to give up some of your fantasies if you're going to be a useful janitor. *(Exits.)*

K. *(Notices the Assistants.)* Yes, what is it?

JEREMIAH. We thought you should know —

ARTHUR. That Herr Klamm is back at the Manor House —

JEREMIAH. He decided not to stay the night —

ARTHUR. He's in a very foul mood —

JEREMIAH. He ordered his sleigh be made ready —

ARTHUR. To return to the Castle —

JEREMIAH. You might just catch him —

ARTHUR. If you hurry —

JEREMIAH. Yes, if you hurry.

FRIEDA. *(Seizing K's arm.)* No, not yet.

K. What do you mean 'not yet'? There are limits, believe me —

FRIEDA. Believe me: There aren't. You'll make it worse —

K. *(Looks in her eyes.)* I understand why you're scared — but I'm not, and that shouldn't frighten you more. *(K gently removes her hand, heads for the exit.)*

37

FRIEDA. *(Shouting after the exiting K.)* You won't be able to see him! He'll refuse! *(K exits.)* Idiot — *(Angrily she looks around, sees the oddly sheepish expressions on the Assistants' faces.)* Well — ?

JEREMIAH. *(To Frieda.)* Let him be. He knows best, Frieda —

ARTHUR. Yes, we'll help you pack — *(The Assistants each take, in turn, one step closer to Frieda, then stop. She looks from one to the other. In spite of herself, her lips curl into a faint smile. She laughs at them. They clear the room; the cube is rotated 45 degrees, so the point no longer faces the audience.)*

Scene 7

Night: in and around a sleigh in the driveway in front of the Manor House. The Coachman sits in a chair in front of the cube, which is the cabin of the sleigh and contains some seats, a blanket and a small flask. K enters on the run, stares at him. Sound of horses snorting, stamping.

K. Does this sleigh belong to Herr Klamm?

COACHMAN. No sir. It belongs to the Castle.

K. *(Pause.)* Will Herr Klamm be driving it up to the Castle then?

COACHMAN. No sir. I'll be driving it. *(K just smiles.)*

K. And you are — ?

COACHMAN. Herr Klamm's driver.

K. I see. *(The Coachman coughs. K claps his arms around himself to keep warm. He walks completely around the sleigh once. Then he leans against its cabin. He stands for a few moments in the cold, shivering and hitting his hands together to warm them.)*

COACHMAN. It might be a long time.

K. What might be a long time?

COACHMAN. Before you go away. *(K stares at the Coachman, not sure if he understood the remark.)*

K. Are there any blankets in the sleigh?

COACHMAN. You'll get me in trouble. *(K opens the door of the*

cabin and gets in. He looks around for blankets.)
COACHMAN. You'll get me in trouble. Get out of there! *(K ignores him and puts the blanket around him. The Coachman climbs down to watch K more carefully.)*
COACHMAN. *(Mumbling.)* A very long time. *(The Coachman turns and exits, heading towards the Manor House. K finds a small flask of alcohol. When he opens it, he hears heavenly music, similar to what he heard over the phone in Scene 2. K lifts the flask to drink, and the music cuts out. He drinks once, then again, and begins to giggle as he drops it accidentally, spilling the liquid all over his seat.)*
K. Damn! *(He wipes furiously at the seat with his hand, then tries to dry his hand on his clothes ... Finally he gives up and drinks what's left from the flask, but it's not much. He curls himself into a ball to keep warm, his feet on the seats, but is unable to get comfortable. He begins to shiver ... Gradually, night becomes dawn. K, still shivering, has not slept. A stern-looking well-dressed man — Momus — enters, followed by the Coachman. Momus peers into the cabin, where he sees K. After a moment, he taps on the cabin door. K sits upright, startled.)*
MOMUS. Come with me.
K. I'm waiting for someone.
MOMUS. I know. Come.
K. I'll miss the person I'm waiting for.
MOMUS. You'll miss him in any case, whether you go or stay.
K. Then I'd rather wait for him and miss him. *(Momus stares at K for a moment, with a hint of a smile on his face.)*
MOMUS. *(Turning to the Coachman.)* Unharness the horses.
COACHMAN. Now, sir?
MOMUS. Now. *(Momus looks again at K, then exits. The Coachman begins to unhook straps from the coach, then walks offstage accompanied by the sound of walking horses. K watches this for a moment — then after a short time, he climbs out of the sleigh and — shivering with each step — heads off in the direction of Momus' exit.)*

Scene 8

In the Bar of the Manor House, moments later. K enters, his face blue with cold. Momus sits at a table, interviewing the Innkeeper's Wife, who stands before him. They stop talking as K enters, shivering.

MOMUS. Ah, the Land-surveyor. At last. Now if I could ask you sir, if you wouldn't mind, to take a moment and answer a few questions that I have here —

K. I'm af-fraid I don't have the time. *(Shivers uncontrollably.)*

MOMUS. I'm sorry, I should've introduced myself: I'm Momus, Herr Klamm's Village Secretary.

K. And what does a V-Village Secretary do, when he's not dealing with horses? *(A sound of neighing horses is heard offstage.)*

MOMUS. *(Over the sound of departing hooves.)* I deal with Herr Klamm's arrivals and departures, naturally. *(K stares dumbfoundedly at him ... then rushes to the window and — clearly watching Klamm's sleigh depart — starts miming banging on the glass in frustration until we hear the glass smash. As the sound of hooves recedes, K whips around and glares at Momus in both rage and despair. K is pale, sweaty, ill. His left hand has been sliced by the glass and bleeds.)*

MOMUS. It's true, Land-surveyor, as soon as you gave up your sentry duty, Herr Klamm was able to leave. *(Lifts a few sheets of paper.)* Now if you don't mind there's only a few short questions here —

K. I'm ... scarcely in the mood for it.

MOMUS. Your janitorial duties beckon?

K. How dare you speak to me that way!

MOMUS. *(Slamming a document on the table.)* In the name of Klamm, I command you to answer the questions!

K. "In the name of Klamm"! Does he trouble himself about my affairs, then?

MOMUS. That's something I wouldn't know. In the meantime, I

command you, by the power vested in me by Herr Klamm himself, to answer the questions!

INNKEEPER'S WIFE. Answer him, Land-surveyor; and if you don't, I refuse to advise you any further. All my good advice has come back to slap me in the face.

K. And what do you have to do with any of this?

INNKEEPER'S WIFE. I've only come here to notify Herr Momus and the administration about your conduct, so I can ensure that I won't be forced to lodge you in my inn again. I will tell you this though: the only way you'll ever get Klamm to even consider your case is by answering the questions here in the secretary's deposition. *(K stares at her in astonishment; turns to Momus.)*

K. *(To Momus.)* Is that correct? If I answer this deposition, will Klamm take the time to read it?

MOMUS. No, why should he? Herr Klamm can't read every deposition — indeed he doesn't read any.

K. Then I refuse to answer the questions.

MOMUS. You absolutely refuse?

K. Without question.

MOMUS. Initial here, *(Rather than sign, K touches his thumb to the paper and, with blood, leaves his thumbprint; Momus is unamused.)* and here, and here and … now we have nothing more to say. *(Momus takes out a rubber stamp and begins to stamp the documents.)*

K. *(After a pause.)* When is Herr Klamm returning here?

INNKEEPER'S WIFE. You think Klamm will speak to you, after you've refused his Secretary!

K. *(To Momus.)* Is that true?

MOMUS. I'm afraid so. This was an important deposition.

K. Even if Klamm doesn't read it?

MOMUS. Even then.

K. Then I suppose I shouldn't have refused.

MOMUS. Initialed and stamped. I'm sorry. *(He turns to leave, stops, turns back to K.)* Still, that doesn't mean that sulphur will come raining down from the sky, or anything like that. *(Momus smiles at K — inexplicably, K smiles back.)* Well, if you'll excuse me, I have to finish this lady's report. *(K stops smiling. Momus waits for K to leave. K just stands there, staring back at him, begins shivering again, now from what seems like fever. Momus turns to the Innkeeper's Wife, sighing.)*

MOMUS. The Land-surveyor seems to have his heart set on remaining here. Perhaps we could finish this elsewhere? *(The Innkeeper's Wife nods, Momus collects his papers, and the pair exit. K shakily sits in Momus' chair, takes out his handkerchief, and — still shivering uncontrollably — wraps it around his bloody hand, wincing. He then lays his head on his arms on the table, shivers again from head to toe ... Behind him, Frieda and the Assistants enter. K does not raise his head.)*

FRIEDA. *(Annoyed.)* Is this where you've been all night, while we were freezing in the schoolhouse? *(Suddenly concerned by his shivering.)* What's the matter — ? *(Takes hold of his face.)* — You're burning up —

K. Why would you be f-freezing in the s-schoolhouse — ?

ARTHUR. Because you got us kicked out of the inn where it was nice and warm —

JEREMIAH. And then we had to sleep on the schoolhouse floor —

ARTHUR. And steal some wood from the woodshed —

JEREMIAH. We broke the lock —

ARTHUR. That part was easy —

JEREMIAH. But of course the schoolteacher got mad —

ARTHUR. In the morning —

JEREMIAH. Since we had to tell him —

ARTHUR. That the Land-surveyor —

JEREMIAH. Had authorized the appropriation —

ARTHUR. EX-propriation —

JEREMIAH. Expropriation —

ARTHUR. Of the wood.

JEREMIAH. We couldn't say it was us.

ARTHUR. He had a stick.

JEREMIAH. He would've beaten us.

ARTHUR. *(To K.)* And so you're fired.

JEREMIAH. That's right! The schoolteacher fired you, Land-surveyor!

ARTHUR. You're out of a job!

JEREMIAH. *(Worried, to Arthur.)* But then so are we.

ARTHUR. *(To Jeremiah.)* And all because he's rude to people —

42

JEREMIAH. Yes, quite rude —

ARTHUR. To important people —

JEREMIAH. Like the mayor —

ARTHUR. And the teacher —

JEREMIAH. And the innkeeper's wife —

ARTHUR. And Klamm's secretary —

JEREMIAH. That's like being rude —

ARTHUR. To Klamm himself!

JEREMIAH. A smart move, Land-surveyor!

ARTHUR. Very strategic! *(K suddenly erupts, takes a flailing swing at Arthur. K misses, which sends him spinning around 180 degrees, landing him in Jeremiah's arms, who throws him back to Arthur. Arthur and Jeremiah then spin and toss him back and forth, as K continues to try to strike at them, unsuccessfully, with his fists.)*

FRIEDA. *(Grabbing at the Assistants, trying to stop them.)* Stop it! Stop it! *(Finally K collapses onto his knees, exhausted, breathing in gasps.)*

K. You're fired ... Both of you.

JEREMIAH. Did you hear that? We're fired.

ARTHUR. *(Shrugging.)* He's the boss! *(The Assistants take off their hats and glasses, and relax their tight shoulders and manic expressions. Suddenly, they appear as though they've just taken off their roles as the Assistants: as though they've just gotten off work. For the first time, they seem like two normal individuals. They walk casually out of the room. K and Frieda sit for a moment, lost in despair.)*

K. Frieda ... Tell me ...

FRIEDA. Yes, darling?

K. Does Klamm still send for you?

FRIEDA. Haven't you learned anything yet?

K. *(Leaning his forehead on hers.)* I don't understand you. I thought you were like me: striving to advance yourself —

FRIEDA. *(Taking his face in her hands again.)* I won't be able to stand this life here. If you want me to stay with you, you'll have to take me away from here.

K. Away?

FRIEDA. Yes.

K. Now — ?

FRIEDA. Yes! Klamm isn't your goal anymore. I've had all I want of Klamm, too much of him! It's to escape from Klamm that I want. We have a much finer life ahead of us …

K. I don't know what to say … *(K suddenly goes faint. Frieda cradles his head in her lap. K lies there with his eyes closed, feverish. Frieda strokes his forehead.)*

FRIEDA. When you're near me like this, I can't imagine anything better than being with you … Without interruption. Without end … I even think … how nice it would be to lie in the grave with you, deep in the grave, side by side … we'll embrace like pliers. I'll hide my face against you, you'll hide yours against me, and nobody will ever see us again … *(K slowly pulls back from her.)*

K. I came here to stay, and I will stay. What could have brought me to this place … other than a desire to stay?

FRIEDA. You're just like Klamm. You have no feelings for me; I'm just a possession to you. Well then, by all means, stay. Messenger! *(Frieda storms out. Barnabas appears, as if summoned. K struggles to his feet.)*

K. Barnabas —

BARNABAS. *(Holding out a letter.)* I'm sorry to interrupt, sir. It's a letter from Klamm —

K. *(Astonished.)* What — *(Leans on Barnabas, takes the letter.)* I can't believe it — an answer — *(K tries to open the envelope, but his hands shake too severely.)* You open it — *(Barnabas — while still supporting K — opens the letter, then hands it to K. Rather than take the letter, K just closes his eyes.)* Read it, please —

BARNABAS. *(Slowly, a bit illiterate.)* "To the Land-surveyor at the Bridge Inn. Your surveying work so far has been excellent. The work of the assistants is also praiseworthy. Don't let anything interfere with your goals until you've brought them to a conclusion. Any interruption would be very disappointing. Rest assured, the question of payment will soon be decided." That's all … *(K looks at Barnabas in confusion.)*

K. Were you given this letter personally by Herr Klamm?

BARNABAS. Yes sir.

K. When?

BARNABAS. Just a little while ago.

K. In the Castle?

BARNABAS. In the Castle. *(K suddenly grabs Barnabas' lapels in a*

vice-like grip, as much out of vehemence as to help him stay on his feet.)
K. Did he say anything when he gave you the letter?
BARNABAS. *(Fearful of the look in K's eye.)* You're not angry with
me, are you sir — ? *(K shakes Barnabas emphatically with almost
every other word of the following:)*
K. I have a message for you to take back to him. Tell him ... that
the Land-surveyor begs Herr Klamm to grant him a personal
interview. He accepts in advance any conditions that may be
attached to the permission to do this. He is driven to make this
request because until now every intermediary has failed. The
Land-surveyor knows how extraordinary his request is, but he will
exert himself ... exert himself ... *(Having spent all his energy on this
attempt to communicate his basic wishes, K collapses in his arms.)*

Scene 9

*In the Barnabas family hut, late afternoon. The stage is
rotated to an off-kilter angle, and the ramshackle furnishings
are set: a table, a faded and fallen tapestry of a crumbling
castle, chairs piled up. K awakens to find himself in a chair
with a blanket over his lap. Olga is sitting next to him, holding a cup and saucer.*

OLGA. Some tea — *(Olga hands him the teacup. K takes it, raises
the cup shakily to his lips.)* You were in an awful state when
Barnabas brought you in. You still have a fever — *(K sips the tea,
winces at the horrible taste, spits it back into the cup.)* — Perhaps
you're not ready to take liquids yet.
K. No, it's that it tastes like ...
OLGA. I'm sorry — we have very little here. *(She takes the teacup
from him.)* My brother only recently got the job of messenger,
Herr Land-surveyor. And even that he does for no pay.
K. But you work at the Manor Inn.
OLGA. If I didn't do that we'd both starve. *(K looks perplexed.)*

Hasn't Frieda told you anything about us?

K. No. But the mere mention of you or your brother seems to enrage her.

OLGA. And the Innkeeper's wife? Did she say anything? *(K shakes his head.)* Or anyone else?

K. No one's said a thing — but the hatred toward you —

OLGA. None of them can bring themselves to speak of it — the fact that we're disgraced. *(Gets up.)* I think once you've heard why, maybe you won't want to have anything to do with us either, Land-surveyor —

K. But how are you "disgraced"? I think I must be the "disgraced" one here —

OLGA. *(Putting teacup on counter.)* Oh no. You still receive letters from Herr Klamm …

K. That's true.

OLGA. *(Draws her chair closer to him.)* Three years ago, a Castle official named Sortini took notice of me —

K. Sortini — ?

OLGA. It was at a celebration that our whole family attended — a party given by the Fire Brigade. This Sortini sent a messenger to our house — which was much finer back then, when our parents were still alive. His message was to me personally: a summons to come to him at the Manor House. But it was written in the most awful, vile language — I'd never seen such words in writing before, and anyone who saw it would've considered the girl it was written to to be the very lowest sort of person there could ever be. It wasn't a love letter, certainly: It was a letter about hunger … written in the language of hatred … I ripped it up and threw it back in the messenger's face.

K. And then?

OLGA. We were one of the wealthiest families in the Village in those days. But, yes, after that night my parents were kept from doing any kind of work. There was hardly any food — my father broke down immediately, he became sick, mentally ill. Both my parents died the next winter. We hired lawyers to try and overturn the case, but they kept telling us they had nothing to go on — especially given my dismissal of Sortini's advances and the insult to his messenger —

K. I'm sorry all of this has happened to you. It's so unjust …

OLGA. You may be the only one in the Village who thinks so, K. *(Suddenly alarmed.)* Now you're pale again —

K. It must be terrible for you. The inhumanity of it —

OLGA. *(Touching his cheek tenderly.)* You're kind to think of me — *(Worried, she moves her hand to his forehead.)*

K. *(Grabbing her hand.)* It's human to do so —

OLGA. All the same, it's an act of kindness on your part …

K. But why do you submit? Why do you let them…?

OLGA. I guess I believe that if the Castle sees to what level one of our family — me, that is — is willing to sink, perhaps they'll forgive the old sin. *(Sound of stomping footsteps offstage.)*

BARNABAS. *(Voice off.)* Land-surveyor! Land-surveyor — ! *(Barnabas bursts in, stomping and brushing, beaming.)* I succeeded!

K. *(Rising, holding onto the back of his chair to steady himself.)* So Klamm will give me my interview?

BARNABAS. Well … no. But I stood right near his desk for almost half a day, and each time Klamm looked up I raised my hand — even though that's forbidden — until finally he left, and then a clerk in his office took a broom and swept me out of the room —

K. *(Crest-fallen.)* That's not success, Barnabas.

BARNABAS. Oh, but it is, sir. As I was leaving the office I saw an official coming down the hall. It was Erlanger, one of Klamm's chief secretaries — if not *the* Chief Secretary. He recognized me at once: "Aren't you Barnabas?" he said. "I was just going to the Manor House. The Land-surveyor is to report to me there. But he must come at once. I've only a few things to settle there and then I leave again for the Castle at five in the morning. Tell him that it's very important that I speak to him."

K. *(Standing wobbily, but his pulse clearly racing.)* You said, "Chief Secretary"?

OLGA. *(To K.)* He's very important, Land-surveyor. Everyone knows who Erlanger is.

K. He's close to Klamm?

BARNABAS. Very close to Klamm. Perhaps no one is closer.

K. Then this is it. This is it. Barnabas —

BARNABAS. *(Noticing that K looks as ill as before.)* Perhaps a longer rest for you sir, before you go —

K. No. You said it was Erlanger. Chief Secretary. An end to the errors. Is this clarity?

OLGA. *(Rising.)* My brother's right, Land-surveyor, wait a little longer —

K. But those aren't the instructions. *(Puts on the coat, heads for the door.)* Those aren't the instructions —

Scene 10

In a Corridor of the Manor House, night. The stage is cleared. K enters, and joins a line of three tired peasants, including the Coachman. K looks dead on his feet. He actually rests his forehead on the back of the Peasant in front of him. Momus enters, walking rapidly.

MOMUS. Ah, the Land-surveyor!

K. How long will it be?

MOMUS. You're here to see — ?

K. Herr Erlanger.

MOMUS. All these people are waiting for Secretary Erlanger —

FIRST PEASANT. I've been here six hours.

K. But I was summoned here personally.

MOMUS. *(To K, ironically.)* The man who was so unwilling to be examined earlier … Follow me. *(Walks him all the way around the cube and leads him to the back of the line.)* Now you're ready.

K. You only think of yourselves — !

MOMUS. *(Over his shoulder, as he exits.)* Of whom, then, should we think? Who else is there? *(Exits.)*

K. *(To the Peasant in front of him.)* Don't you find it odd that we've been summoned here in the middle of the night?

FIRST PEASANT. *(Not turning around.)* We should only be too thankful to Herr Erlanger for seeing us at all.

K. But I tell you, I was summoned here personally —

COACHMAN. *(Joining the line behind K.)* You're still in the Village?

K. *(Turning around.)* Yes. I've come here for good.

COACHMAN. *(Shaking his head.)* That doesn't matter to me.

K. *(Staring at the Coachman a moment — suddenly he takes him by the arm, tries to take him aside.)* Listen —

COACHMAN. *(Resisting being taken out of line.)* Don't take me out of line —

K. I want to make a trade with you —

COACHMAN. Leave me alone, will you —

K. I want to give up my place in line to you — for a ride up the hill. In your sleigh.

COACHMAN. *(In a loud voice, so all can hear.)* You want to trade your place in line for a ride up to the Castle?

K. Shh shhh! I didn't say that. *(Frieda suddenly walks by, wearing an apron, carrying a jug of water.)* Frieda — ? *(Frieda ignores K, keeps walking. K stares after her, stunned to see her here — he runs after her, grabs her by the elbow.)* Frieda —

FRIEDA. *(Not looking him in the eye.)* I'm busy, I can't talk now —

K. You're *here?* *(Frieda gradually turns, looks at him — she notices with shock his deteriorated condition. Instinctively her hands rise to comfort him — but she resists the impulse, looks away from his gaze.)*

FRIEDA. I've been taken on in the taproom again. Not as the full barmaid, but I'm hoping to get my position back.

K. I've been pushing so hard ...

FRIEDA. I'll bring you a chair.

K. I don't want a chair, Frieda —

JEREMIAH. *(Voice off.)* Frieda — ? *(Jeremiah enters, wearing a wrap/compress around his head.)* Land-surveyor? *(Frieda disengages herself from K, steps away, as Jeremiah approaches and puts a hand on one of Frieda's shoulders.)* As you can see I got sick from our night in the schoolhouse. But I shouldn't complain: Arthur was much more upset. He filed a complaint against you in the Castle. I'd watch out for him if I were you.

K. And you?

JEREMIAH. Arthur's putting in a complaint for me as well.

K. What do you have to complain about?

JEREMIAH. That you can't take a joke. *(Jeremiah suddenly sneezes into both his hands, then blows his nose in a hanky. K looks stunned by the truth about Jeremiah and Frieda.)* But you look awful: why don't you come lie down in our room for a while? You and Frieda probably have things to talk about, and I won't be in the way. I know how it is when two people break up, the things they want to say to each other before saying goodb — What — ? *(Frieda has jerked Jeremiah by the arm, and now drags him along with her, away from K.)*

FRIEDA. That's enough! Enough! *(Frieda drags Jeremiah offstage, exiting. K is now alone on a bare stage. He looks around, starts shivering again from fever. The line of people waiting for Erlanger seems to have disappeared. K begins to walk, inside the cube, as the cube spins in the opposite direction, faster and faster. The music builds as K runs around in circles until finally he collapses in the middle of the cube as it comes to a halt.)*

VOICE. *(Booming, offstage.)* Is the Land-surveyor there?

K. *(Looking around.)* Yes! *(Momus enters, stops, looks at his watch impatiently.)*

VOICE. *(Offstage.)* Then tell him it's high time for him to come out here!

K. Yes yes! *(Looking around wildly, desperate; he sees Momus.)* Who was that?

MOMUS. *(Harsh whisper.)* Erlanger, of course — go to him at once! He's already annoyed, try to placate him!

K. Yes — but where?

MOMUS. Outside —

K. Outside — ?

MOMUS. In his sleigh: Make haste!

VOICE. Land-surveyor!

MOMUS. Why are you just standing there?

K. I —

MOMUS. If you delay any longer, Erlanger will come down on *me* —

K. No, of course, I —

MOMUS. *(Taking K by the elbow and steering him rapidly toward the exit.)* Who knows what awaits you there: everything here is an opportunity — except that some opportunities are too great for any of us to take advantage of ... Well, get going! *(A storm surrounds K: He is outside.)*

Scene 11

Night: the driveway in front of the Manor House. Erlanger strides across the stage. K follows and stops him.

K. Herr Erlanger!

ERLANGER. You should have come long ago, Land-surveyor.

K. *(Out of breath.)* I'm terribly sorry, Herr Secretary, I was unable to find your room —

ERLANGER. *(Closes his eyes.)* I don't want any excuses, stop it please — *(A pause; he opens his eyes again.)* What I need to tell you is this: formerly a certain Frieda was employed in the taproom. I only know her name, I don't know the girl herself. At any rate, this Frieda served beer to Herr Klamm from time to time. Now there seems to be another girl there. Well: this change is probably of no importance to anyone, and certainly it's of no importance to Herr Klamm. But the bigger a job is — and Herr Klamm's job is, of course, the biggest — the more disturbing any little changes or alterations in the routine can be. For example, the smallest alteration on a desk, the shifting of an inkwell even half an inch, all this can be fairly disturbing; and so, in the same way, a new barmaid can be, as well. *(Erlanger eyes K, waiting for a response.)*

K. Yes!

ERLANGER. This Frieda must at once return to the taproom. You're living with her I'm told. Therefore: arrange immediately for her return.

K. Yes!

ERLANGER. — If I'm able to report that you've shown yourself reliable in this affair, it could be of use to you at some point in the future, with regard to the improvement of your prospects. That's all I have to say. *(Erlanger nods a nod of dismissal to K, clearly finished with the conversation. Two Coachmen place chairs facing the audience at the lip of the stage, and position themselves behind the chairs facing away. These chairs are the two seats in the open sleigh.*

51

Erlanger sits. K, on the other hand, stands there in shock ... then suddenly sinks to his knees, tears filling his eyes, his arms outstretched to Erlanger, or the sky.)

K. *(In pure agony.)* In the name of *Klamm,* wait!

ERLANGER. *(Turns, now in the sleigh.)* Eh? What's that?

K. Mercy, your honor, I beg you to show me some mercy!

ERLANGER. *(Narrowing his eyes.)* And how am I going to do that, I'd like to know —

K. By giving me a ride, sir: by giving me a place beside you — there — beside you, sir ... *(Erlanger stares at K a moment — his expression becomes faintly bemused, with the ghost of a smile perhaps, but not unsympathetic.)*

ERLANGER. It's a ride to the Castle you want?

K. Yes sir.

ERLANGER. Are you sure, Land-surveyor?

K. Yes. A thousand times. Yes sir, yes ... *(Erlanger looks back at K, thinks ...)*

ERLANGER. No. I can't —

K. *(Getting to his feet.)* Please!

ERLANGER. I can't be responsible —

K. *(Grabbing Erlanger's arm.)* Listen to me: I'll swear to anyone who asks that the responsibility was mine! And you'll gain in me, sir, from this day forward, a faithful servant, a devoted slave, who'll not only execute your wishes sir, but who'll *anticipate* those wishes, in ways that will expand the concept of service so far beyond its present definition that it might better be said to approximate the ongoing dedication that some venture to call *love,* sir — if you take my meaning ... *(Erlanger looks at K for a while, immovable. Finally he sighs.)*

ERLANGER. It won't do you any good, of course ... *(Pause.)* And I think I've warned you — in fact I'm sure I have, but ... All right. Sit. *(K, startled by the word, doesn't move.)* Sit, Land-surveyor. *(K quickly sits beside Erlanger in the sleigh. To the Second Coachman.)* Drive on! *(The Second Coachman cracks the whip.)*

Scene 12

We are riding in the sleigh with K and Erlanger. They face us. The sound of the horses, the creak of the harnesses, the wind — all is heard atmospherically throughout the following. A curtain closes behind K and Erlanger, separating them from the scenery change to come.

K is slumped next to Erlanger — looking too exhausted, perhaps, to enjoy where he is. There's a pause before Erlanger speaks.

ERLANGER. Your case reminds me of a story that we tell up here sometimes, Land-surveyor. It tells of events that happened a long time ago — that is, if they happened at all. It's a tale you might find illuminating. Perhaps my telling it will shorten the journey?

K. That would be nice.

ERLANGER. It's about a man — not unlike yourself — who tried to gain entrance to the Castle, many years ago ... *(The curtain opens behind them, revealing the tall forbidding doors of the Castle instead of the open cube. K and Erlanger stand and remove their chairs to the sides of the stage. K now becomes the "man" of the parable, standing before these doors, enacting or speaking as Erlanger (in shadow) narrates. An eerie, haunting music replaces the sound of the storm.)*

ERLANGER. The story has it that the man arrived one day to find the Castle gates locked and barred — *(K knocks on the Castle doors — a sound effect booms. A Gatekeeper emerges, wearing a fur, with a long Tartaric beard. He closes the door behind him, stands guard.)*

ERLANGER. The man begs for admittance. But the gatekeeper says:

GATEKEEPER. I can't admit you at the moment.

K. Will I be allowed to enter later?

GATEKEEPER. It's possible. But not now. If you're tempted, you may try to force your way past me. But I'm only the lowest gate-

53

keeper. From hall to hall, gatekeepers stand at every door, each one more powerful than the last. Already the sight of the third of these men is more than even I can stand.

ERLANGER. Such difficulties the man had not expected, but he decides he had better wait, lest he bring the gatekeeper's wrath down upon his head. The gatekeeper gives him a little stool and lets him rest. *(It happens.)* There the man sits waiting for days and years, wearying the gatekeeper with his importunity. The gatekeeper often engages him in brief conversation, but it always ends with the statement:

GATEKEEPER. I'm sorry but you cannot be allowed to enter yet.

ERLANGER. The man, who has equipped himself with many things for his journey, parts with all he has, however valuable, in the hope of bribing the gatekeeper. *(It happens.)* The gatekeeper accepts it all, saying:

GATEKEEPER. I take this only to keep you from feeling that you've left something undone —

ERLANGER. And during all the long years the man forgets about what lies beyond this gatekeeper, as this one seems to him the only barrier between himself and the Castle. In the first years the man curses his fate; but later, as he grows old, his eyes grow dim, and he can't be sure whether the world is really darkening around him or whether it's his eyes that are deceiving him. But in the darkness he can now perceive a radiance that streams inextinguishably from the doors of the Castle ... *(It happens.)* Now his life draws to a close, and it's at that moment, right before he dies, that everything he's experienced condenses in his mind into a single question. He motions to the gatekeeper to come closer:

GATEKEEPER. What do you want now? You're insatiable —

K. Why?

GATEKEEPER. Why what?

K. Why can't I get though the door?

GATEKEEPER. That is not for me to answer.

K. Then who? If not you, who?!

GATEKEEPER. Who else is there?

K. There's only me and you.

ERLANGER. The gatekeeper perceives that the man is nearing his end, so he bends down further to speak in his ear:

54

GATEKEEPER. If you'll permit me then — as we've come to the end here — I must now lock this door for good. You can look, if you like, while I go ... Goodbye. *(As the Gatekeeper opens the door, the light floods our eyes — then the Gatekeeper goes into the Castle. As he closes the door with a boom, the theater goes dark and the music which has been underscoring this parable — which we now realize has been that faraway sound of humming from Scene 2 — crescendos to a climax ... only to be replaced in the dark with the sound of the storm and the horses pulling the sleigh. The curtain closes, leaving K and Erlanger sitting side by side in the sleigh as before.)*

K. So the gatekeeper deceived the man.

ERLANGER. I don't know if one could say that.

K. It's clear enough. The gatekeeper told the man that he couldn't "admit him at the moment," implying that he would at some future time.

ERLANGER. Ah. But he never could admit him "at that moment."

K. But the man never got inside; it's very unjust.

ERLANGER. Of course it's just. The man is really free, he can go where he likes, it's only the Castle that's closed to him. When he sits by the door and stays there for the rest of his life, he does it of his own free will.

K. But to gain admittance, that was all he wanted ... And that was his right.

ERLANGER. It was his right to *try*.

K. But what does that mean?

ERLANGER. Land-surveyor, it's only a story. Told to shorten your journey. *(K considers this for a long moment.)*

K. I've spent everything I have, to get to the Castle and be a part of it.

ERLANGER. And what if the Castle, as you think of it, doesn't exist?

K. That's a terrible thing to say to me! That's a terrible thing! Of course it exists!

ERLANGER. Well then ... maybe it does.

K. Well, which is it? What am I to accept as the truth? *(We hear the Coachman say "Whoa," as the horses and sleigh come to a halt. Only the sound of the wind remains, desolate and unrelenting. The curtain opens, but instead of the Castle doors we saw previously, there's only the open stage with the hollow cube in a desolate, wintry landscape as at the top of the play.)*

ERLANGER. Ah, here we are. I can't take you any further, I'm afraid. *(Pause.)* You'll have to get out here.

K. Are we here? Can't you take me inside with you?

ERLANGER. I'm not getting out here. *(Pause.)* And, unfortunately, I'm not going back.

K. I see. *(K nods, rises, gets out of the sleigh.)* May I enter the Castle here?

ERLANGER. I'm afraid I don't know.

K. If so — will there be a gatekeeper to let me in?

ERLANGER. *(Smiles.)* I'm afraid I don't know that either. I've never tried to enter this way.

K. And how long will I have to wait?

ERLANGER. Well ... there are paths that lead away from here, through the trees. If you get too cold, you might see where one of them leads. But now I really must be going. I have work yet to do before sunrise. *(To the Coachman we don't see.)* Drive on! (*Again, the sound of a whip and of departing horses. Lights down on Erlanger as he and his "sleigh" disappear from view ... K is left alone ... He turns to see what awaits him. We see the image from the beginning of the play. K is looking at a clearing in the snowy woods, with a strange, otherworldly glass box in its center. K sighs, but smiles a little. Slowly he approaches the box, trudging in his exhaustion, a gait that reminds us of the play's opening image.*

With what seems like great effort, K reaches up and knocks. But this time, unlike in the play's beginning, no sound accompanies his gesture. Instead, his hand falls through the "wall" into the cube: There are no walls or doors at all.

K steps into into the middle of the box. A light snow begins to fall over him, but only inside the cube. He shivers for a moment, but then looks up into the descending flakes. A beam of sunlight pierces through the darkness, turning the snowfall into a gentle rain of sparkling light. K smiles.

Finally K sits, facing us, and closing his eyes, he turns his face upward to receive the falling snow, a look of pure bliss on his face. Very gradually, K lowers his head until it appears to rest on his chest. The

56

snow continues to fall but only on his motionless body. After a pause, Barnabas enters.)

BARNABAS. Herr Land-surveyor — I bring wonderful news … *(A pause: K does not respond.)* They've finally offered me a job: as an office servant, with pay! — And I have good news for you as well, sir: You've received official permission to live in the Village — I've been looking all over for you so I could tell you … *(K is motionless.)* There are certain limitations, of course, but still: real permission! *(Barnabas' smile of joy at being the bearer of such good news very gradually evaporates … With a look of concern he goes closer to K.)* Herr Land-surveyor…? *(Barnabas is about to enter the cube to nudge/wake K … but he stops just at its invisible wall, as if thinking better of it. Barnabas remains outside the cube for a moment longer, staring at the motionless K, on whom snow continues to fall … Finally, Barnabas turns away, pauses a moment, then exits. Lights slowly fade to black. The snow never stops falling on the motionless K.)*

End of Play

PROPERTY LIST

Beers (PEASANTS, INNKEEPER'S WIFE)
Glasses and a dish towel (INNKEEPER'S WIFE)
Mattress and horse blanket (K)
Old-fashioned phone receiver (INNKEEPER, ASSISTANTS, K)
Basin and soap, hand-towel (INNKEEPER'S WIFE)
Coat (K)
Guestbook and pen (INNKEEPER)
Plate of fold (INNKEEPER)
Snowballs (ARTHUR, JEREMIAH)
Letter (BARNABAS, K)
Horsewhip (FRIEDA, COACHMAN)
Chairs (MAYOR, COACHMAN)
Small stool (MAYOR, GATEKEEPER)
Boxes of Files (ARTHUR, JEREMIAH)
Watch (TEACHER)
Hat (TEACHER)
Seats, blankets, flask with liquid (COACHMAN)
Document (MOMUS)
Blood (K)
Handkerchief (K, JEREMIAH)
Rubber stamp (MOMUS)
New letter (BARNABAS)
Blanket (K)
Cup and saucer (OLGA)
Apron, jug of water (FRIEDA)
Head compress (JEREMIAH)

SOUND EFFECTS

Wind, snowstorm-louder, then softer
Knocking on a wooden door
Phone ringing
Heavenly humming, far away
Voice on phone (Oswald)
Phone hang-up
Lovemaking
Birdsong
Neighing horses
Departing hooves
Smashing glass
Music
Horses
Loud knocking
Horses stopping and sleigh
Horses and sleigh departing

The Castle
Set Design by Anna Louizos

Audience Seating

Spotlights

Revolving Square Platform
(Suspended over center turning mechanism)

Snowbanks/Trees

Path

Entrances/Steps

NEW PLAYS

★ **BE AGGRESSIVE by Annie Weisman.** Vista Del Sol is paradise, sandy beaches, avocado-lined streets. But for seventeen-year-old cheerleader Laura, everything changes when her mother is killed in a car crash, and she embarks on a journey to the Spirit Institute of the South where she can learn "cheer" with Bible belt intensity. "...filled with lingual gymnastics...stylized rapid-fire dialogue..." *–Variety.* "...a new, exciting, and unique voice in the American theatre..." *–BackStage West.* [1M, 4W, extras] ISBN: 0-8222-1894-1

★ **FOUR by Christopher Shinn.** Four people struggle desperately to connect in this quiet, sophisticated, moving drama. "...smart, broken-hearted...Mr. Shinn has a precocious and forgiving sense of how power shifts in the game of sexual pursuit...He promises to be a playwright to reckon with..." *–NY Times.* "A voice emerges from an American place. It's got humor, sadness and a fresh and touching rhythm that tell of the loneliness and secrets of life...[a] poetic, haunting play." *–NY Post.* [3M, 1W] ISBN: 0-8222-1850-X

★ **WONDER OF THE WORLD by David Lindsay-Abaire.** A madcap picaresque involving Niagara Falls, a lonely tour-boat captain, a pair of bickering private detectives and a husband's dirty little secret. "Exceedingly whimsical and playfully wicked. Winning and genial. A top-drawer production." *–NY Times.* "Full frontal lunacy is on display. A most assuredly fresh and hilarious tragicomedy of marital discord run amok...absolutely hysterical..." *–Variety.* [3M, 4W (doubling)] ISBN: 0-8222-1863-1

★ **QED by Peter Parnell.** Nobel Prize-winning physicist and all-around genius Richard Feynman holds forth with captivating wit and wisdom in this fascinating biographical play that originally starred Alan Alda. "QED is a seductive mix of science, human affections, moral courage, and comic eccentricity. It reflects on, among other things, death, the absence of God, travel to an unexplored country, the pleasures of drumming, and the need to know and understand." *–NY Magazine.* "Its rhythms correspond to the way that people—even geniuses—approach and avoid highly emotional issues, and it portrays Feynman with affection and awe." *–The New Yorker.* [1M, 1W] ISBN: 0-8222-1924-7

★ **UNWRAP YOUR CANDY by Doug Wright.** Alternately chilling and hilarious, this deliciously macabre collection of four bedtime tales for adults is guaranteed to keep you awake for nights on end. "Engaging and intellectually satisfying...a treat to watch." *–NY Times.* "Fiendishly clever. Mordantly funny and chilling. Doug Wright teases, freezes and zaps us." *–Village Voice.* "Four bite-size plays that bite back." *–Variety.* [flexible casting] ISBN: 0-8222-1871-2

★ **FURTHER THAN THE FURTHEST THING by Zinnie Harris.** On a remote island in the middle of the Atlantic secrets are buried. When the outside world comes calling, the islanders find their world blown apart from the inside as well as beyond. "Harris winningly produces an intimate and poetic, as well as political, family saga." *–Independent (London).* "Harris' enthralling adventure of a play marks a departure from stale, well-furrowed theatrical terrain." *–Evening Standard (London).* [3M, 2W] ISBN: 0-8222-1874-7

★ **THE DESIGNATED MOURNER by Wallace Shawn.** The story of three people living in a country where what sort of books people like to read and how they choose to amuse themselves becomes both firmly personal and unexpectedly entangled with questions of survival. "This is a playwright who does not just tell you what it is like to be arrested at night by goons or to fall morally apart and become an aimless yet weirdly contented ghost yourself. He has the originality to make you feel it." *–Times (London).* "A fascinating play with beautiful passages of writing..." *–Variety.* [2M, 1W] ISBN: 0-8222-1848-8

DRAMATISTS PLAY SERVICE, INC.
440 Park Avenue South, New York, NY 10016 212-683-8960 Fax 212-213-1539
postmaster@dramatists.com www.dramatists.com

NEW PLAYS

★ **SHEL'S SHORTS by Shel Silverstein.** Lauded poet, songwriter and author of children's books, the incomparable Shel Silverstein's short plays are deeply infused with the same wicked sense of humor that made him famous. "...[a] childlike honesty and twisted sense of humor." –*Boston Herald.* "...terse dialogue and an absurdity laced with a tang of dread give [*Shel's Shorts*] more than a trace of Samuel Beckett's comic existentialism." –*Boston Phoenix.* [flexible casting] ISBN: 0-8222-1897-6

★ **AN ADULT EVENING OF SHEL SILVERSTEIN by Shel Silverstein.** Welcome to the darkly comic world of Shel Silverstein, a world where nothing is as it seems and where the most innocent conversation can turn menacing in an instant. These ten imaginative plays vary widely in content, but the style is unmistakable. "...[*An Adult Evening*] shows off Silverstein's virtuosic gift for wordplay...[and] sends the audience out...with a clear appreciation of human nature as perverse and laughable." –*NY Times.* [flexible casting] ISBN: 0-8222-1873-9

★ **WHERE'S MY MONEY? by John Patrick Shanley.** A caustic and sardonic vivisection of the institution of marriage, laced with the author's inimitable razor-sharp wit. "...Shanley's gift for acid-laced one-liners and emotionally tumescent exchanges is certainly potent..." –*Variety.* "...lively, smart, occasionally scary and rich in reverse wisdom." –*NY Times.* [3M, 3W] ISBN: 0-8222-1865-8

★ **A FEW STOUT INDIVIDUALS by John Guare.** A wonderfully screwy comedy-drama that figures Ulysses S. Grant in the throes of writing his memoirs, surrounded by a cast of fantastical characters, including the Emperor and Empress of Japan, the opera star Adelina Patti and Mark Twain. "Guare's smarts, passion and creativity skyrocket to awesome heights..." –*Star Ledger.* "...precisely the kind of good new play that you might call an everyday miracle...every minute of it is fresh and newly alive..." –*Village Voice.* [10M, 3W] ISBN: 0-8222-1907-7

★ **BREATH, BOOM by Kia Corthron.** A look at fourteen years in the life of Prix, a Bronx native, from her ruthless girl-gang leadership at sixteen through her coming to maturity at thirty. "...vivid world, believable and eye-opening, a place worthy of a dramatic visit, where no one would want to live but many have to." –*NY Times.* "...rich with humor, terse vernacular strength and gritty detail..." –*Variety.* [1M, 9W] ISBN: 0-8222-1849-6

★ **THE LATE HENRY MOSS by Sam Shepard.** Two antagonistic brothers, Ray and Earl, are brought together after their father, Henry Moss, is found dead in his seedy New Mexico home in this classic Shepard tale. "...His singular gift has been for building mysteries out of the ordinary ingredients of American family life..." –*NY Times.* "...rich moments ...Shepard finds gold." –*LA Times.* [7M, 1W] ISBN: 0-8222-1858-5

★ **THE CARPETBAGGER'S CHILDREN by Horton Foote.** One family's history spanning from the Civil War to WWII is recounted by three sisters in evocative, intertwining monologues. "...bittersweet music—[a] rhapsody of ambivalence...in its modest, garrulous way...theatrically daring." –*The New Yorker.* [3W] ISBN: 0-8222-1843-7

★ **THE NINA VARIATIONS by Steven Dietz.** In this funny, fierce and heartbreaking homage to *The Seagull*, Dietz puts Chekhov's star-crossed lovers in a room and doesn't let them out. "A perfect little jewel of a play..." –*Shepherdstown Chronicle.* "...a delightful revelation of a writer at play; and also an odd, haunting, moving theater piece of lingering beauty." –*Eastside Journal (Seattle).* [1M, 1W (flexible casting)] ISBN: 0-8222-1891-7

DRAMATISTS PLAY SERVICE, INC.
440 Park Avenue South, New York, NY 10016 212-683-8960 Fax 212-213-1539
postmaster@dramatists.com   www.dramatists.com